Teaching Little Fingers to Play

Classics

Piano Solo Arrangements
With Optional Teacher Accompaniments

by

Randall Hartsell

CONTENTS

Cover Design by Nick Gressle

© 2001 by The Willis Music Company
International Copyright Secured
Printed in the USA

12397

Rests

In music notation there are SIGNS of SILENCE, called RESTS, which tell us when and for how long our fingers should be silent.

QUARTER REST 𝄽 = 1 count

WHOLE REST* ▬ = 4 counts in this piece!

*The WHOLE REST receives the counts for the whole measure indicated by the top number of the time signature.

Eighth Notes

The time value of an eighth note ♪ is HALF as long as that of a quarter note. Play TWO eighth notes to one count.

Student Position

One Octave Higher When Performing as a Duet

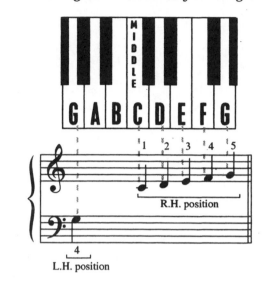

Ode to Joy
(from Symphony No. 9)

Optional Teacher Accompaniment

Ludwig van Beethoven
Arr. Randall Hartsell

Ode to Joy

(from Symphony No. 9)

Play both hands one octave higher when performing as a duet.

Ludwig van Beethoven
Arr. Randall Hartsell

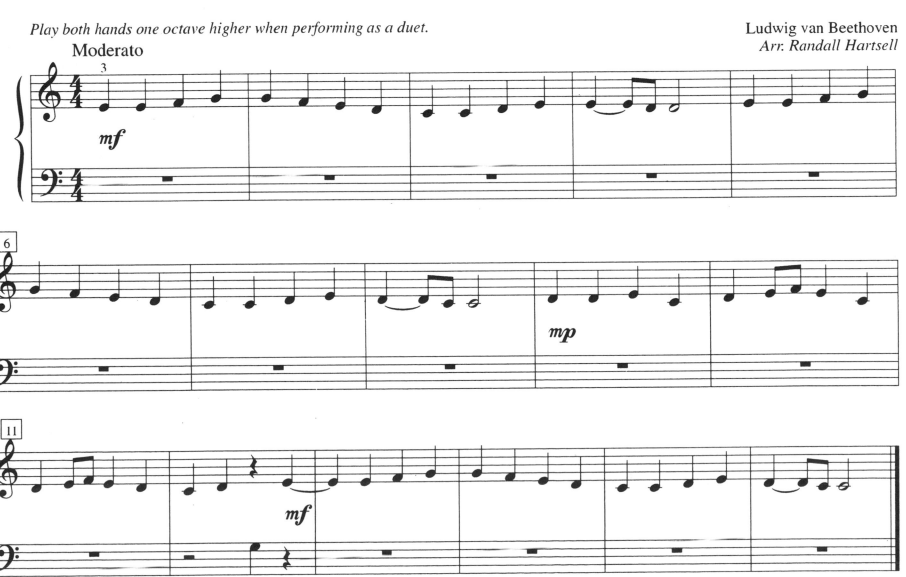

12397

The Dotted Half Note 𝅗𝅥.
(THREE-BEAT NOTE)
HOLD FOR 3 BEATS (1, 2, 3)
A DOT after a note increases
the value of that note by one half.

Dynamics
DYNAMICS are suggestions by the
composer to help create contrasts in
your music. Watch for the *loud* (𝆑)
in this piece.

Student Position
One Octave Higher When Performing as a Duet

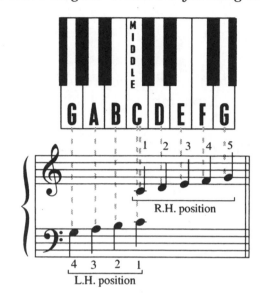

A Little Night Music
(from *Eine kleine Nachtmusik*)

Optional Teacher Accompaniment

Wolfgang Amadeus Mozart
Arr. Randall Hartsell

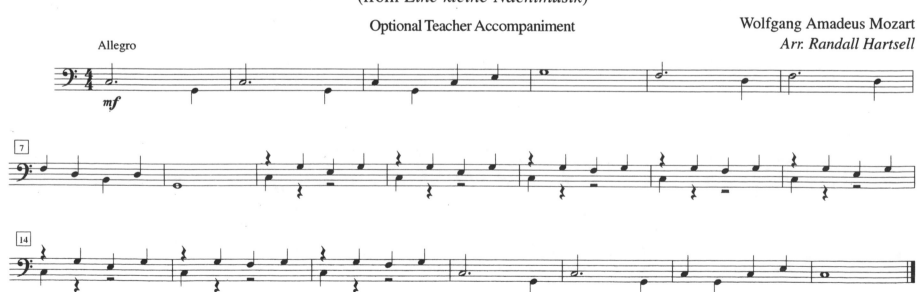

A Little Night Music

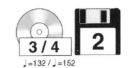

(from *Eine kleine Nachtmusik*)

Play both hands one octave higher when performing as a duet.

Wolfgang Amadeus Mozart
Arr. Randall Hartsell

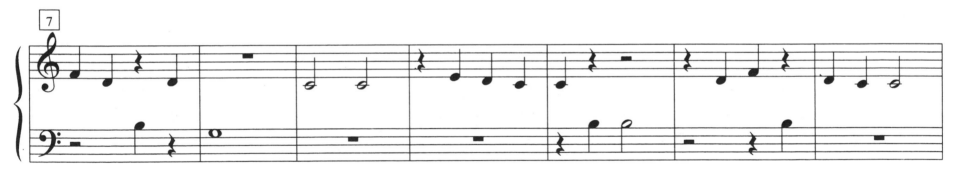

12397

Staccato

When a note has a dot under or over it, play the key like it's "hot"! The Italian word for this is STACCATO and it means to play crisply and detached.

Accidentals

A SHARP or FLAT placed next to a note but not found in the key signature is called an ACCIDENTAL and only changes the pitch for the measure in which it occurs.

Student Position

One Octave Higher When Performing as a Duet

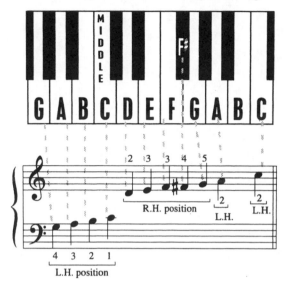

"Surprise" Symphony

Optional Teacher Accompaniment

Joseph Haydn
Arr. Randall Hartsell

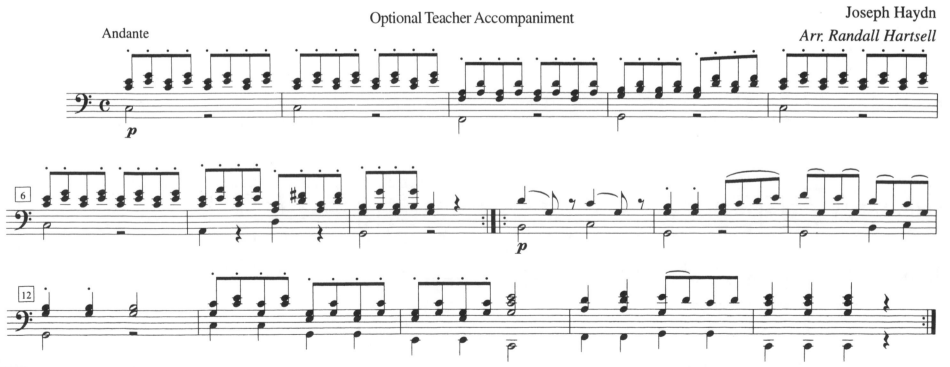

"Surprise" Symphony

Joseph Haydn

Arr. Randall Hartsell

Play both hands one octave higher when performing as a duet.

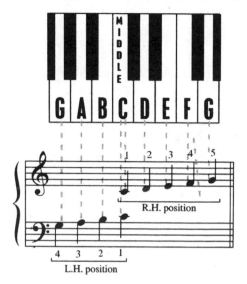

Student Position
One Octave Higher When Performing as a Duet

Crescendo - Decrescendo

When you see these

gradually get louder then gradually get softer.

Bridal Chorus
(from *Lohengrin*)

Optional Teacher Accompaniment

Richard Wagner
Arr. Randall Hartsell

Bridal Chorus

(from *Lohengrin*)

7 / 8   4

♩=100 / ♩=120

Play both hands one octave higher when performing as a duet.

Richard Wagner
Arr. Randall Hartsell

Moderato

The Tie

The TIE is a curved line joining one note to another of the SAME PITCH. Play the first note and hold for the value of both.

Student Position
One Octave Higher When Performing as a Duet

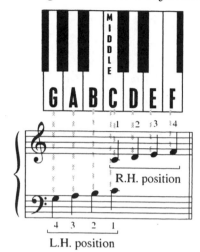

Symphony No. 5
(Second Movement)

Optional Teacher Accompaniment

Peter Ilyich Tchaikovsky
Arr. Randall Hartsell

Symphony No. 5
(Second Movement)

Play both hands one octave higher when performing as a duet.

Peter Ilyich Tchaikovsky

Arr. Randall Hartsell

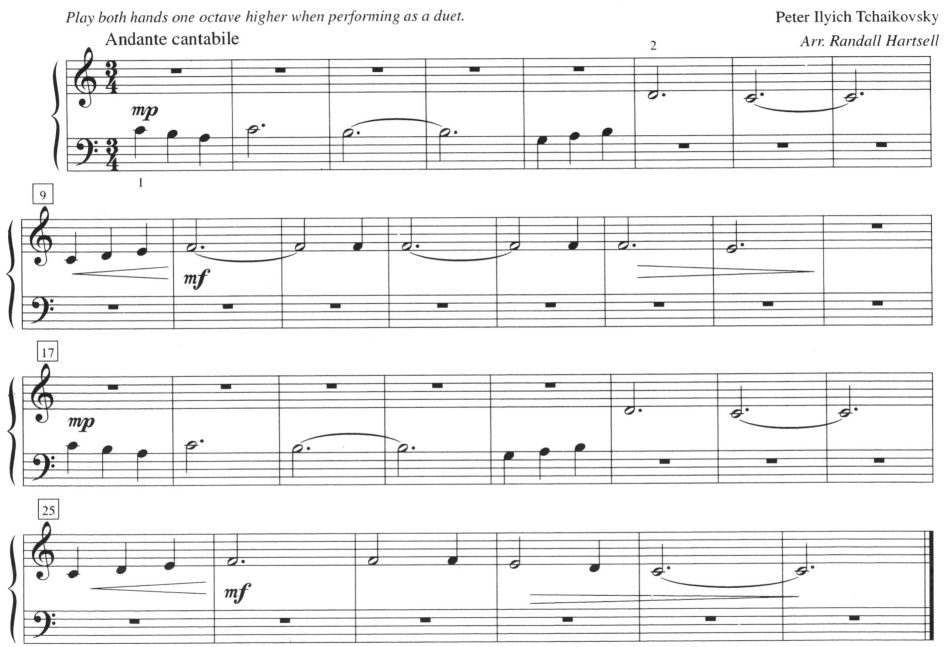

12397

Ritardando

This means to gradually slow down.

Student Position

One Octave Higher When Performing as a Duet

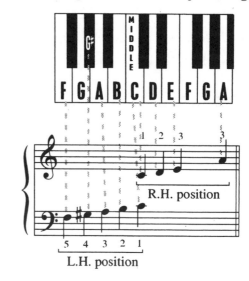

Swan Lake

Optional Teacher Accompaniment

Peter Ilyich Tchaikovsky
Arr. Randall Hartsell

Allegro

ritardando

Swan Lake

Peter Ilyich Tchaikovsky

Arr. Randall Hartsell

Play both hands one octave higher when performing as a duet.

Patterns

Groups of notes that are repeated in a PATTERN can help you to memorize your piece. Practice the patterns first, then put it all together.

Student Position
One Octave Higher When Performing as a Duet

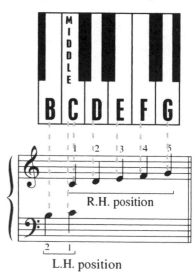

Barcarolle
(from *Tales of Hoffman*)

Optional Teacher Accompaniment

Jacques Offenbach
Arr. Randall Hartsell

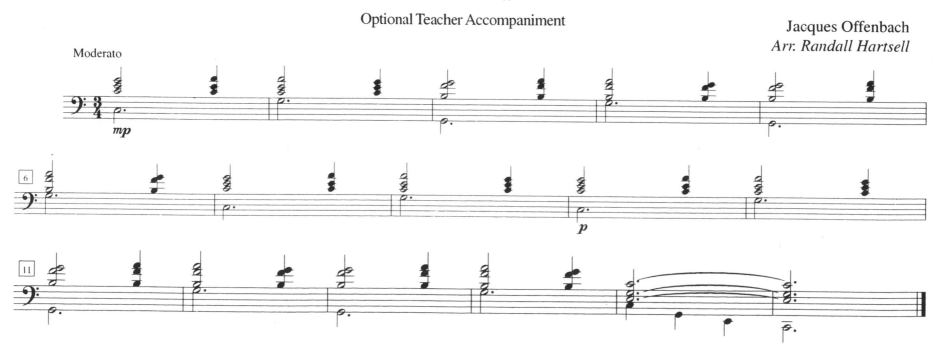

Barcarolle
(from the Opera *Tales of Hoffman*)

Play both hands one octave higher when performing as a duet.

Jacques Offenbach
Arr. Randall Hartsell

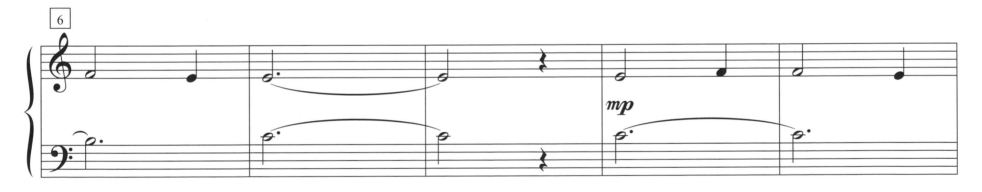

Key Signature

When the SHARP sign (♯) is placed between the clef sign and the time signature it becomes the KEY SIGNATURE. In this piece all F's must be sharped. (Play the first black key to the right of F.)

Student Position
One Octave Higher When Performing as a Duet

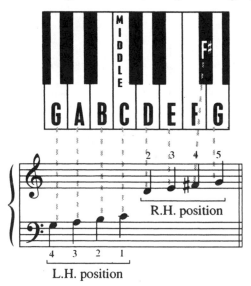

Can-Can
(from *Orpheus in the Underworld*)

Optional Teacher Accompaniment

Jacques Offenbach
Arr. Randall Hartsell

Can-Can

(from *Orpheus in the Underworld*)

Jaques Offenbach
Arr. Randall Hartsell

Play both hands one octave higher when performing as a duet.

An Incomplete Measure

This piece begins on beat THREE.
You must accent the first beat AFTER
the bar line.

Student Position

One Octave Higher When Performing as a Duet

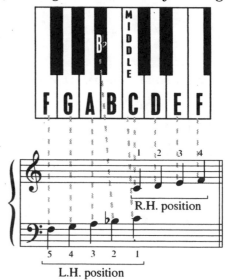

Key Signature

When the FLAT sign (♭) is placed between the clef
sign and the time signature it becomes the KEY
SIGNATURE. In this piece all B's must be flatted.
(Play the first black key to the left of B.)

Lullaby

Optional Teacher Accompaniment

Johannes Brahms
Arr. Randall Hartsell

Lullaby

Johannes Brahms

Arr. Randall Hartsell

Play both hands one octave higher when performing as a duet.

The Phrase

Groups of notes, like words in books, tell stories when they are arranged in 'sentences' and punctuated. A curved line over a group of notes indicates a MUSICAL SENTENCE called a PHRASE.

Student Position

One Octave Higher When Performing as a Duet

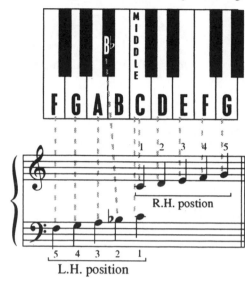

Country Gardens

Optional Teacher Accompaniment

English Folk Tune
Arr. Randall Hartsell

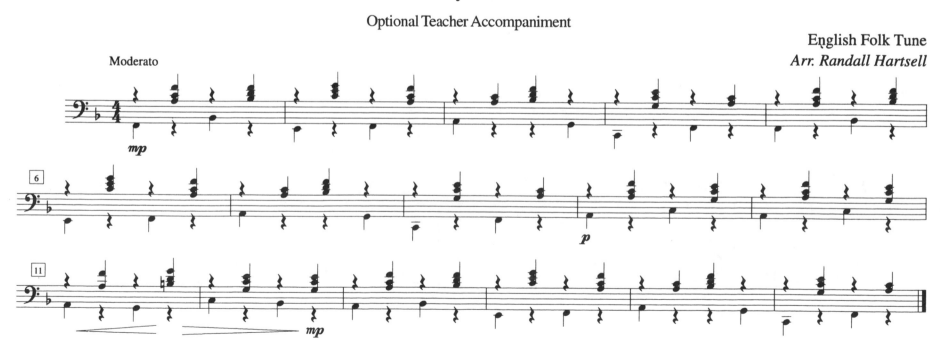

Country Gardens

Play both hands one octave higher when performing as a duet.

English Folk Tune
Arr. Randall Hartsell

Moderato

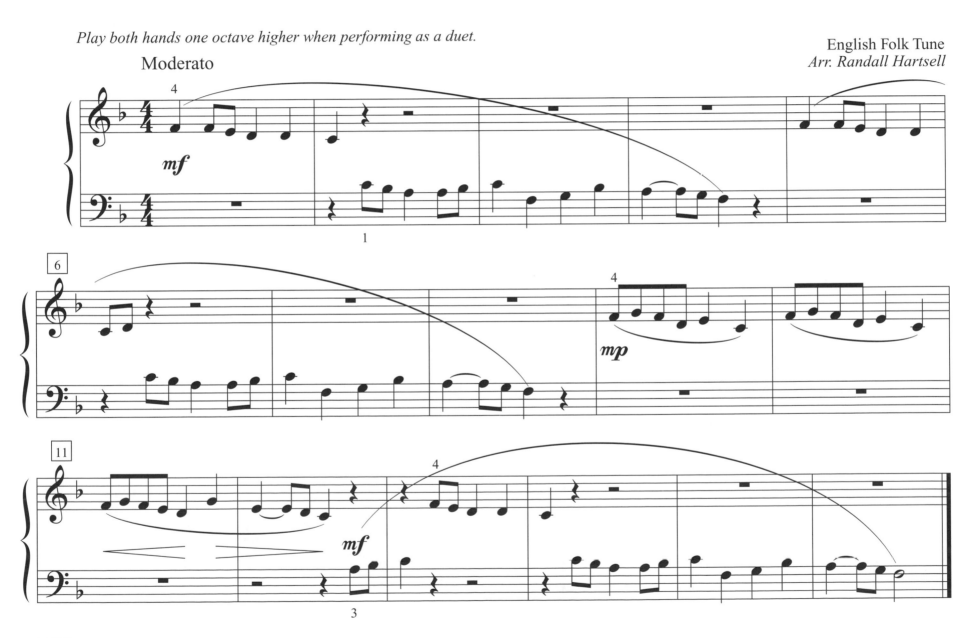

Student Position
One Octave Higher When Performing as a Duet

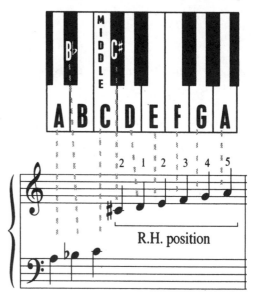

Dynamics
DYNAMICS are suggestions made by the composer to help create contrasts in your music. Watch for the *mf* in this piece. It means mezzo forte or medium loud. The *mp* means mezzo piano or medium soft.

Turkish March
(from *The Ruins of Athens*)

Optional Teacher Accompaniment

Ludwig van Beethoven
Arr. Randall Hartsell

Turkish March

(from *The Ruins of Athens*)

Play both hands one octave higher when performing as a duet.

Ludwig van Beethoven
Arr. Randall Hartsell

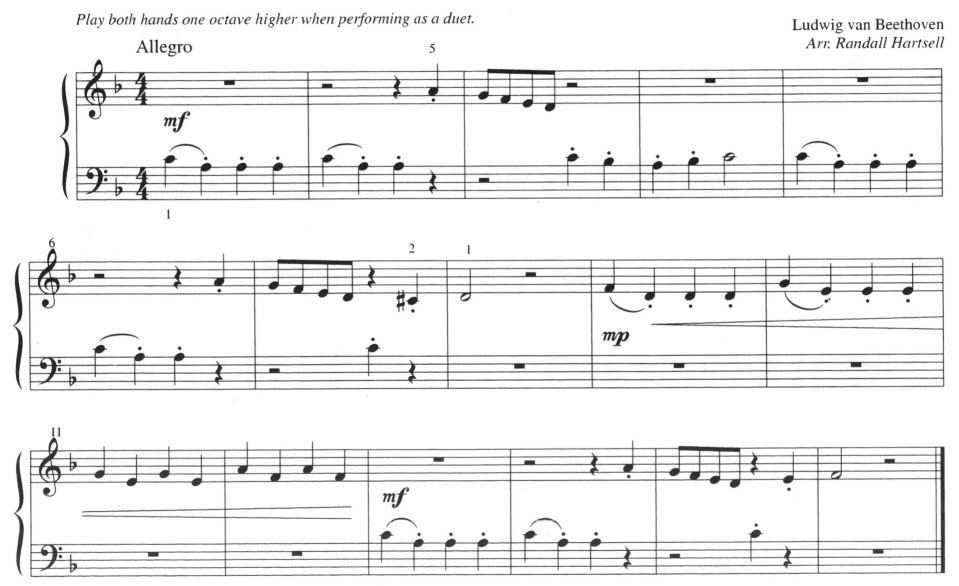

Teaching Little Fingers To Play....
EVERYTHING THEY **WANT** TO PLAY!

Starting from the very beginning with *Teaching Little Fingers To Play* by John Thompson and progressing through *Teaching Little Fingers To Play More* by Leigh Kaplan, students will enjoy practicing and performing these wonderful supplements!

If it's **FUN** to **PLAY**...
It's *Teaching Little Fingers*!